God's Little
Instruction Book
for Teens

HONOR
B O O K S

07 06 05 04 03   10 9 8 7 6 5 4 3 2 1

God's Little Instruction Book for Teens
ISBN 1-56292-799-X
Copyright (c) 1998, 2003 by Honor Books
An Imprint of Cook Communcations Ministries
4050 Lee Vance View
Colorado Springs, CO 80918
www.cookministries.com

Get Fired Up!

You haven't quite made it all the way into the world of adults, but you're almost there—and you sure aren't a kid anymore!

New issues and challenges face you every day. Where do you turn for advice? How do you get fired up when you're feeling a little knocked down?

God's Little Instruction Book for Teens is a great source of wisdom and encouragement to help you meet life head on—not just get by—with poise, style, integrity, and faith.

Take the powerful quotes and scriptures found in this handy little book to heart. You will be well on your way to making an incredible difference in your world!

Many receive advice; only the wise profit by it.

Pride only breeds quarrels, but wisdom
is found in those who take advice.
— Proverbs 13:10 NIV

The only way to have a friend is to be one.

A man that hath friends must
shew himself friendly.

— Proverbs 18:24

The world wants your best, but God wants your all.

"Thou shalt love the Lord thy God
with all thy heart, and with all
thy soul, and with all thy mind."

— Matthew 22:37

A Christian must keep the faith, but not to himself.

"Go ye into all the world, and preach the gospel to every creature."

— Mark 16:15

No horse gets anywhere

until he is harnessed.

No life ever grows great

until it is focused,

dedicated, disciplined.

In a race, everyone runs but only one person
gets first prize. . . . To win the contest you
must deny yourselves many things that
would keep you from doing your best.

— 1 Corinthians 9:24-25 TLB

♪ have never been

hurt by anything

♪ didn´t say.

Don't talk so much. You keep

putting your foot in your mouth.

Be sensible and turn off the flow!

— Proverbs 10:19 TLB

We too often love

things and use people,

when we should be

using things and

loving people.

Be devoted to one another in brotherly love.

Honor one another above yourselves.

— Romans 12:10 NIV

When you flee temptations, don't leave a forwarding address.

Now flee from youthful lusts and
pursue righteousness ... with those who
call on the Lord from a pure heart.

— 2 Timothy 2:22 NASB

Whatever you dislike

in another person,

take care to correct

in yourself.

"Why do you look at the speck of sawdust
in your brother's eye and pay no attention
to the plank in your own eye?"

— Matthew 7:3 NIV

Shoot for the moon.

Even if you miss it

you will land among

the stars.

Aim for perfection.

— 2 Corinthians 13:11 NIV

The secret of success is to do the common things uncommonly well.

Seest thou a man diligent in his business?

he shall stand before kings;

he shall not stand before mean men.

— Proverbs 22:29

Definition of status:
Buying something you
don't need with money
you don't have to impress
people you don't like.

They do all their deeds to be noticed by men.

— Matthew 23:5 NASB

∫ like the dreams

of the future

better than the

history of the past.

Remember ye not the former things,

neither consider the things of old.

Behold, I will do a new thing.

— Isaiah 43:18-19

The way to get to the top is to get off your bottom.

How long will you lie down, O sluggard?

When will you arise from your sleep?

— Proverbs 6:9 NASB

You are only what you are when no one is looking.

Not with eye-service, as men-pleasers;
but as the servants of Christ, doing
the will of God from the heart.

— Ephesians 6:6

There are times when

silence is golden,

other times it is

just plain yellow.

To every thing there is a season . . . a time
to keep silence, and a time to speak.

— Ecclesiastes 3:1-7

A true friend never

gets in your way

unless you happen

to be going down.

If one falls down, his friend can
help him up. But pity the man who
falls and has no one to help him up!

— Ecclesiastes 4:10 NIV

Every job is a self-portrait of the person who does it. Autograph your work with excellence.

Daniel was preferred above the
presidents and princes, because
an excellent spirit was in him.

— Daniel 6:3

The best things

in life are

not free.

Forasmuch as ye know that ye
were not redeemed with corruptible
things, as silver and gold . . . but with
the precious blood of Christ, as of a
lamb without blemish and without spot.

— 1 Peter 1:18-19

23

You can lead

a boy to college,

but you cannot

make him think.

It is senseless to pay tuition to educate
a rebel who has no heart for truth.

— Proverbs 17:16 TLB

If a man cannot be a

Christian in the place

where he is, he cannot

be a Christian anywhere.

Don't work hard only when your master is
watching and then shirk when he isn't
looking; work hard and with gladness all
the time, as though working for Christ,
doing the will of God with all your hearts.

— Ephesians 6:6-7 TLB

Don't ask God for what you think is good; ask Him for what He thinks is good for you.

"After this manner therefore pray ye . . .
Thy kingdom come. Thy will be done
in earth, as it is in heaven."

— Matthew 6:9-10

Opportunities

are seldom

labeled.

Seek, and ye shall find; knock,
and it shall be opened unto you.

— Matthew 7:7

The wise does at once what the fool does at last.

He that gathereth in summer is a
wise son: but he that sleepeth in
harvest is a son that causeth shame.

— Proverbs 10:5

Nothing great

was ever

achieved without

enthusiasm.

The joy of the LORD is your strength.

— Nehemiah 8:10

Trust in yourself and you are doomed to disappointment; but trust in God, and you are never to be confounded in time or eternity.

It is better to take refuge in the Lord than to trust in man.

— Psalm 118:8 NIV

Don't be discouraged;

everyone who got

where he is, started

where he was.

Though your beginning was insignificant,
yet your end will increase greatly.

— Job 8:7 NASB

Maturity doesn't come with age; it comes with acceptance of responsibility.

When I was a child, I spake as a child,
I understood as a child, I thought
as a child: but when I became a man,
I put away childish things.

— 1 Corinthians 13:11

The man who wins may have been counted out several times, but he didn't hear the referee.

Though a righteous man falls
seven times, he rises again.
— Proverbs 24:16 NIV

The happiest people don't necessarily have the best of everything. They just make the best of everything.

I have learned, in whatsoever state I am, therewith to be content. I can do all things through Christ which strengtheneth me.

— Philippians 4:11,13

Keep company

with good men

and good men

you will imitate.

Iron sharpeneth iron; so a man sharpeneth

the countenance of his friend.

— Proverbs 27:17

Learn by

experience—

preferably other

people's.

All these things happened to them as
examples—as object lessons to us—
to warn us against doing the same things.

— 1 Corinthians 10:11 TLB

Many men have too much will power. It's won't power they lack.

A man without self-control is as defenseless
as a city with broken-down walls.
— Proverbs 25:28 TLB

It's not hard

to make decisions

when you know what

your values are.

Daniel purposed in his heart that
he would not defile himself.

— Daniel 1:8

Conquer yourself rather than the world.

Encourage the young men
to be self-controlled.

— Titus 2:6 NIV

I am only one; but still
I am one. I cannot do
everything, but still I can do
something; I will not refuse
to do the something I can do.

Under his direction the whole body is fitted
together perfectly, and each part in its
own special way helps the other parts.

— Ephesians 4:16 TLB

Politeness goes far, yet costs nothing.

A kind man benefits himself.

— Proverbs 11:17 NIV

We should behave to our friends as we would wish our friends to behave to us.

"As ye would that men should do to you,
do ye also to them likewise."

— Luke 6:31

Who ceases

to be a friend,

never was one.

This people honors Me with their lips,

but their heart is far away from Me.

— Mark 7:6 NASB

Character is

what you are

in the dark.

The integrity of the upright

shall guide them.

— Proverbs 11:3

Adversity

causes some men

to break; others

to break records.

If thou faint in the day of adversity,

thy strength is small.

— Proverbs 24:10

Learn to say "No";

it will be of more

use to you than to be

able to read Latin.

Just say a simple yes or no,
so that you will not sin.

— James 5:12 TLB

A man who wants

to lead the orchestra

must turn his

back on the crowd.

Wherefore come out from among them, and be
ye separate, saith the Lord, and touch not
the unclean thing; and I will receive you.

— 2 Corinthians 6:17

Men are alike in their promises. It is only in their deeds that they differ.

Many a man claims to have unfailing love,
but a faithful man who can find?
— Proverbs 20:6 NIV

Don't cross your bridges

until you get to them.

We spend our lives

defeating ourselves

crossing bridges

we never get to.

Don't be anxious about tomorrow.

God will take care of your tomorrow too.

Live one day at a time.

— Matthew 6:34 TLB

He that has learned to obey will know how to command.

The wise in heart accept commands,
but a chattering fool comes to ruin.

— Proverbs 10:8 NIV

You must have long-range goals to keep you from being frustrated by short-range failures.

Let us fix our eyes on Jesus, the author
and perfecter of our faith, who for
the joy set before him endured the cross,
scorning its shame, and sat down at the
right hand of the throne of God.

— Hebrews 12:2 NIV

Clear your mind of can't.

I can do all things through Christ
which strengtheneth me.

— Philippians 4:13

The future

belongs to those

who believe in the

beauty of their dreams.

"Anything is possible if you have faith."

— Mark 9:23 TLB

The future belongs

to those who see

possibilities before

they become obvious.

The vision is yet for an appointed time . . .
it will surely come, it will not tarry.

— Habakkuk 2:3

When I was a young man I observed that nine out of ten things I did were failures. I didn't want to be a failure, so I did ten times more work.

He becometh poor that dealeth with a slack hand: but the hand of the diligent maketh rich.

— Proverbs 10:4

To recognize opportunity is the difference between success and failure.

Make the most of every opportunity.

— Colossians 4:5 NIV

Jumping to conclusions

is not half as good

an exercise as digging

for facts.

Study to shew thyself approved unto God,

a workman that needeth not to be ashamed,

rightly dividing the word of truth.

— 2 Timothy 2:15

The most valuable of
all talents is that of
never using two words
when one will do.

In the multitude of words there wanteth not
sin: but he that refraineth his lips is wise.

— Proverbs 10:19

Laziness is often mistaken for patience.

Let us lay aside every weight, and the sin
which doth so easily beset us, and let us run
with patience the race that is set before us.

— Hebrews 12:1

One-half the trouble
of this life can be
traced to saying "yes"
too quick, and not
saying "no" soon enough.

Seest thou a man that is hasty in his words?
there is more hope of a fool than of him.

— Proverbs 29:20

I would rather fail in the cause that someday will triumph than triumph in a cause that someday will fail.

Now thanks be unto God, which always
causeth us to triumph in Christ.

— 2 Corinthians 2:14

Carve your name

on hearts and not

on marble.

The only letter I need is you yourselves!
They can see that you are a letter from
Christ, written by us. . . . not one
carved on stone, but in human hearts.

— 2 Corinthians 3:2,3 TLB

A knowledge of the

Bible without a college

course is more valuable

than a college course

without the Bible.

All scripture is given by inspiration of God,
and is profitable for doctrine, for reproof, for
correction, for instruction in righteousness:
that the man of God may be perfect,
thoroughly furnished unto all good works.

— 2 Timothy 3:16-17

Little minds are tamed

and subdued by

misfortune; but great

minds rise above them.

A just man falleth seven times,
and riseth up again.

— Proverbs 24:16

There is no poverty that can overtake diligence.

He becometh poor that dealeth
with a slack hand: but the hand
of the diligent maketh rich.

— Proverbs 10:4

Never despair;

but if you do,

work on in despair.

Be strong and do not give up,
for your work will be rewarded.

— 2 Chronicles 15:7 NIV

You can accomplish

more in one hour

with God than one

lifetime without Him.

"With God all things are possible."

— Matthew 19:26

If you don't stand for something, you'll fall for anything!

If you do not stand firm in your faith,
you will not stand at all.

— Isaiah 7:9 NIV

The difference

between ordinary

and extraordinary

is that little extra.

Whatsoever thy hand findeth to do,

do it with thy might.

— Ecclesiastes 9:10

Man cannot discover new oceans unless he has the courage to lose sight of the shore.

Peter got out of the boat, and walked
on the water and came toward Jesus.

— Matthew 14:29 NASB

Fads come and go; wisdom and character go on forever.

O my son, be wise and stay in God's paths.

— Proverbs 23:19 TLB

Perseverance is a great element of success; if you only knock long enough and loud enough at the gate, you are sure to wake up somebody.

"Ask, and it shall be given you; seek, and ye shall find; knock, and it shall be opened unto you."

— Luke 11:9

Consider the postage stamp: its usefulness consists in the ability to stick to one thing till it gets there.

I have fought a good fight, I have finished my course, I have kept the faith.

— 2 Timothy 4:7

It needs more skill than I can tell to play the second fiddle well.

He that is greatest among
you shall be your servant.

— Matthew 23:11

A man never discloses

his own character so

clearly as when he

describes another's.

A good man out of the good treasure
of the heart bringeth forth good things:
and an evil man out of the evil treasure
bringeth forth evil things.

— Matthew 12:35

The greatest use of life is to spend it for something that will outlast it.

Store up for yourselves treasures in heaven,
where moth and rust do not destroy, and
where thieves do not break in and steal.

— Matthew 6:20 NIV

Every man's work, whether
it be literature, or music,
or pictures, or architecture,
or anything else, is always
a portrait of himself.

As in water face reflects face, so
the heart of man reflects man.

— Proverbs 27:19 NASB

What we do on some great occasion will probably depend on what we already are; and what we are will be the result of previous years of self-discipline.

I keep under my body, and bring it into subjection.
— 1 Corinthians 9:27

Our deeds determine us, as much as we determine our deeds.

Even a child is known by his actions, by whether his conduct is pure and right.

— Proverbs 20:11 NIV

What you do speaks so loud that I cannot hear what you say.

Show me your faith without deeds, and
I will show you my faith by what I do.

— James 2:18 NIV

All virtue is summed up in dealing justly.

He hath shewed thee, O man, what is good;
and what doth the Lord require of thee,
but to do justly, and to love mercy,
and to walk humbly with thy God?

— Micah 6:8

No matter what a man's past may have been, his future is spotless.

Forgetting those things which are behind, and reaching forth unto those things which are before.

— Philippians 3:13

One of Life's

great rules is this:

The more you give,

the more you get.

The liberal soul shall be made fat:
and he that watereth shall
be watered also himself.

— Proverbs 11:25

Everything comes to him who hustles while he waits.

We do not want you to become lazy, but
to imitate those who through faith and
patience inherit what has been promised.

— Hebrews 6:12 NIV

A well-trained memory

is one that permits

you to forget

everything that isn't

worth remembering.

Whatsoever things are true, whatsoever

things are honest, whatsoever things are

just . . . if there be any virtue, and if

there be any praise, think on these things.

— Philippians 4:8

Defeat is not the worst of failures. Not to have tried is the true failure.

Be strong and of a good courage;
be not afraid, neither be thou dismayed:
for the LORD thy God is with thee
whithersoever thou goest.

— Joshua 1:9

Unless you try to

do something beyond

what you have already

mastered, you will

never grow.

Reaching forth unto those things which are
before, I press toward the mark for the prize
of the high calling of God in Christ Jesus.

— Philippians 3:13-14

I don't know the secret

to success, but the key

to failure is to try

to please everyone.

Am I now trying to win the
approval of men, or of God?
— Galatians 1:10 NIV

Kites rise highest against the wind, not with it.

When the way is rough, your patience has a chance to grow. So let it grow, and don't try to squirm out of your problems.

— James 1:3-4 TLB

The secret of success is to be like a duck— smooth and unruffled on top, but paddling furiously underneath.

I laboured more abundantly than
they all: yet not I, but the
grace of God which was with me.

— 1 Corinthians 15:10

The cheerful man will do more in the same time, will do it better, will preserve it longer, than the sad or sullen.

When a man is gloomy, everything seems to go wrong; when he is cheerful, everything seems right!

— Proverbs 15:15 TLB

Money is a good servant but a bad master.

The rich ruleth over the poor, and the
borrower is servant to the lender.

— Proverbs 22:7

No plan is worth the

paper it is printed on

unless it starts you

doing something.

Be ye doers of the word, and not hearers
only, deceiving your own selves.

— James 1:22

Life is a coin. You can spend it any way you wish, but you can spend it only once.

As it is appointed unto men once to die, but after this the judgment.

— Hebrews 9:27

Only passions,

great passions, can

elevate the soul

to great things.

What things soever ye desire, when
ye pray, believe that ye receive
them, and ye shall have them.

— Mark 11:24

Failures want pleasing methods, successes want pleasing results.

No discipline seems pleasant at the time,
but painful. Later on, however, it produces
a harvest of righteousness and peace
for those who have been trained by it.

— Hebrews 12:11 NIV

Once a word has been allowed to escape, it cannot be recalled.

Let no corrupt communication proceed
out of your mouth, but that which is
good to the use of edifying, that it
may minister grace unto the hearers.

— Ephesians 4:29

Most of the things

worth doing in the world

had been declared

impossible before

they were done.

"With God all things are possible."

— Matthew 19:26

Obstacles are those

frightful things you

see when you take your

eyes off the goal.

So Peter . . . walked on the water toward
Jesus. But when he looked around at the high
waves, he was terrified and began to sink.

Matthew 14:29-30 TLB

A good reputation is more valuable than money.

A good name is rather to be
chosen than great riches.

— Proverbs 22:1

An error doesn't become a mistake until you refuse to correct it.

He who heeds discipline shows the
way to life, but whoever ignores
correction leads others astray.

— Proverbs 10:17 NIV

Hating people is like burning down your own house to get rid of a rat.

If ye bite and devour one another, take heed
that ye be not consumed one of another.

— Galatians 5:15

Laughter is the sun that drives winter from the human face.

A merry heart maketh a cheerful
countenance: but by sorrow of
the heart the spirit is broken.

— Proverbs 15:13

Good nature begets smiles, smiles beget friends, and friends are better than a fortune.

The light in the eyes (of him whose heart is joyful) rejoices the heart of others.

— Proverbs 15:30 AMP

No person was ever

honored for what he

received. Honor has

been the reward

for what he gave.

The righteous give without sparing.

— Proverbs 21:26 NIV

The difference between the right word and the almost right word is the difference between lightning and the lightning bug.

A word fitly spoken is like apples of gold in pictures of silver.

— Proverbs 25:11

This world belongs to

the man who is wise

enough to change

his mind in the

presence of facts.

Whoever heeds correction

gains understanding.

— Proverbs 15:32 NIV

Do not remove a fly from your friend's forehead with a hatchet.

Reprove, rebuke, exhort, with great patience and instruction.

— 2 Timothy 4:2 NASB

Every calling

is great when

greatly pursued.

I press toward the mark for the prize of
the high calling of God in Christ Jesus.

— Philippians 3:14

Treat everybody alike,
no matter from what station
in life he comes . . . really
great men and women are those
who are natural, frank, and
honest with everyone with
whom they come into contact.

Don't show favoritism.

— James 2:1 NIV

'Tis better to

be alone, than in

bad company.

Do not be misled: "Bad company
corrupts good character."

— 1 Corinthians 15:33 NIV

The rotten

apple spoils

his companion.

He that walketh with wise men shall be wise:
but a companion of fools shall be destroyed.

— Proverbs 13:20

Patience is bitter but its fruit is sweet.

Ye have need of patience, that,
after ye have done the will of God,
ye might receive the promise.
— Hebrews 10:36

Motivation

is when your

dreams put on

work clothes.

Whatever you do, work at it with all your
heart, as working for the Lord, not for men.

— Colossians 3:23 NIV

Not only to say the right

thing in the right place,

but far more difficult, to

leave unsaid the wrong thing

at the tempting moment.

Self-control means controlling the tongue!

A quick retort can ruin everything.

— Proverbs 13:3 TLB

School seeks to

get you ready for

examination; life

gives the finals.

Examine yourselves to see whether you
are in the faith; test yourselves.

— 2 Corinthians 13:5 NIV

Diligence is
the mother of
good fortune.

The plans of the diligent lead to profit.
— Proverbs 21:5 NIV

The road to
success is dotted
with many tempting
parking places.

Let us lay aside every weight, and the sin
which doth so easily beset us, and let us run
with patience the race that is set before us.

— Hebrews 12:1

When you are laboring

for others let it be with

the same zeal as if it

were for yourself.

Each of you should look not only
to your own interests, but
also to the interests of others.

— Philippians 2:4 NIV

The Bible knows nothing
of a hierarchy of labor.
No work is degrading.
If it ought to be done,
then it is good work.

To rejoice in his labour;
this is the gift of God.

— Ecclesiastes 5:19

The ripest peach is highest on the tree.

Let us not become weary in doing good,
for at the proper time we will reap
a harvest if we do not give up.

— Galatians 6:9 NIV

When you do the things
you have to do when you
have to do them, the day will
come when you can do the
things you want to do when
you want to do them.

He becometh poor that dealeth
with a slack hand: but the hand
of the diligent maketh rich.

— Proverbs 10:4

A man without mirth is
like a wagon without
springs, he is jolted
disagreeably by every
pebble in the road.

A merry heart doeth good like a medicine:
but a broken spirit drieth the bones.

— Proverbs 17:22

The two most important
words: "Thank you."
The most important word:
"We."
The least important word:
"I."

Don't be selfish. . . . Be humble, thinking
of others as better than yourself.

— Philippians 2:3 TLB

Here's the key to

success and the key

to failure: we become

what we think about.

Whatsoever things are true, whatsoever
things are honest . . . if there be any
virtue, and if there be any praise,
think on these things.

— Philippians 4:8

Always bear in mind that your own resolution to success is more important than any other one thing.

The Lord God will help me; therefore
shall I not be confounded: therefore
have I set my face like a flint, and
I know that I shall not be ashamed.

— Isaiah 50:7

Triumph is just "umph" added to try.

Whatsoever thy hand findeth to do,

do it with thy might.

— Ecclesiastes 9:10

A goal properly set is halfway reached.

The LORD answered me, and said, Write the
vision, and make it plain upon tables,
that he may run that readeth it.

— Habakkuk 2:2

I think the one lesson

I have learned is that

there is no substitute

for paying attention.

We ought to give the more earnest heed
to the things which we have heard,
lest at any time we should let them slip.

— Hebrews 2:1

A good listener

is not only popular

everywhere, but

after a while he

knows something.

The ear that heareth the reproof
of life abideth among the wise.

— Proverbs 15:31

When you were born, you
cried and the world rejoiced.
Live your life in such a
manner that when you die the
world cries and you rejoice.

The memory of the righteous
will be a blessing.

— Proverbs 10:7 NIV

Success is never final;

failure is never fatal;

it is courage

that counts.

Be of good courage, and he shall strengthen
your heart, all ye that hope in the LORD.
— Psalm 31:24

$\int$ count him braver

who overcomes his

desires than him who

conquers his enemies; for

the hardest victory is

the victory over self.

I beat my body and make it my slave.

— 1 Corinthians 9:27 NIV

Vision is the world's most desperate need. There are no hopeless situations, only people who think hopelessly.

Where there is no vision, the people perish.

— Proverbs 29:18

People are lonely because they build walls instead of bridges.

You should be like one big happy
family ... loving one another with
tender hearts and humble minds.

— 1 Peter 3:8 TLB

Forgiveness means giving up your right to punish another.

When you stand praying, if you
hold anything against anyone,
forgive him, so that your Father in
heaven may forgive you your sins.

— Mark 11:25 NIV

The most important single ingredient in the formula of success is knowing how to get along with people.

See that no one pays back evil for evil,
but always try to do good to each
other and to everyone else.

— 1 Thessalonians 5:15 TLB

Everyone thinks of changing the world, but no one thinks of changing himself.

"Unless you change and become
like little children, you will
never enter the kingdom of heaven."

— Matthew 18:3 NIV

Courage is resistance to fear, mastery of fear— not absence of fear.

Yea, though I walk through the
valley of the shadow of death, I will
fear no evil: for thou art with me;
thy rod and thy staff they comfort me.

— Psalm 23:4

Prayer is an invisible tool which is wielded in a visible world.

The weapons of our warfare are not carnal, but mighty through God to the pulling down of strong holds.

— 2 Corinthians 10:4

Money is like an arm or leg: use it or lose it.

"To him who has will more be given . . .
and he will have great plenty;
but from him who has not, even the
little he has will be taken away."

— Matthew 13:12 TLB

$\int$n trying

times, don't

quit trying.

The righteous also shall hold on his way,
and he that hath clean hands
shall be stronger and stronger.

— Job 17:9

Let us not say, "Every man is the architect of his own fortune"; but let us say, "Every man is the architect of his own character."

Till I die I will not remove mine integrity
from me. My righteousness I hold fast,
and will not let it go: my heart shall
not reproach me so long as I live.

— Job 27:5-6

It is impossible for

that man to despair

who remembers that his

Helper is omnipotent.

I will lift up my eyes to the mountains;

from whence shall my help come?

My help comes from the LORD,

who made heaven and earth.

— Psalm 121:1-2 NASB

Service is

nothing but love

in work clothes.

The more lowly your service
to others, the greater you are.
To be the greatest, be a servant.

— Matthew 23:11 TLB

Those who have done nothing in life are not qualified to be the judge of those who have done little.

"Judge not, and ye shall not
be judged: condemn not, and
ye shall not be condemned."

— Luke 6:37

People, places, and

things were never meant

to give us life. God

alone is the author

of a fulfilling life.

"I am come that they might have life, and
that they might have it more abundantly."

— John 10:10

COMMON COURTESIES FOR TEENS

"Treat others the same way
you want them to treat you."

—Luke 6:31 NASB

Always say "thank you" when you receive a favor, and say "excuse me" or "pardon me" when needing to interrupt a discussion.

Always knock and

ask permission

before entering

someone's room.

Don't put your feet up on furniture. Feet do not enhance the look of the desk or the table.

Always RSVP

promptly to

every invitation

you receive.

Return anything

borrowed on time,

and in good or better

condition than received.

Be on time for
appointments; leave on time,
too, for nothing is more
boring than someone who
overstays his welcome.

When you dial a wrong number, say, "I'm sorry, excuse me"–instead of slamming down the receiver in the other person's ear.

Acknowledgments

Publius Syrus (5,100), R. W. Emerson (6,29,80), Jim
Patrick (8), H. E. Fosdick (9,102), Calvin Coolidge
(10,105), Sprat (13), Les Brown (14), John Rockefeller,
Jr. (15), Dr. Eugene Swearingen (16,18), Thomas
Jefferson (17,58), Robert C. Edward (19), Ed Cole
(20,32,140), Arnold Glasow (21), Kin Hubbard (24),
Henry Ward Beecher (25,123), John A. Shedd (27,37),
Dwight L. Moody (30,44), H. E. Jansen (33), Roy Disney
(38), Descartes (39), Helen Keller (40), Seneca (41),
Aristotle (42,81,133), William A. Ward (45), Charles H.
Spurgeon (46,62), Moliere (48), Bob Bales (49), Solon
(50), Charles C. Noble (51), Samuel Johnson (52,146),
Eleanor Roosevelt (53), John Sculley (54), George
Bernard Shaw (55), Benjamin Franklin (60,112),
Woodrow Wilson (61), William Lyon Phelps (63),
Washington Irving (64), Terence (66), Henry Wadsworth
Longfellow (72), Josh Billings (73), Jean Paul Richter
(75), William James (76), Samuel Butler (77), H. P.
Liddon (78), George Elliot (78), John R. Rice (82),
William H. Danforth (83,93,110), Thomas Edison (84),
Orlando Battista (85,101), George Woodberry (86),
Ronald E. Osborn (87), Bill Cosby (88), Winston
Churchill (89,132), Thomas Carlyle (91), Bacon (92),
Lillian Dickson (92), Denis Diderot (95), Earl
Nightingale (96,125), Horace (97), Louis D. Brandeis
(98), Hannah More (99), Victor Hugo (103), David Dunn
(104), Mark Twain (106,139), Roy L. Smith (107), Chinese
Proverb (108), Oliver Wendell Holmes (109), George
Washington (111), Parks Robinson (114), George Sala
(115), Say (116), Cervantes (117), Ben Patterson (120),
James Riley (121), Zig Ziglar (122,128), Abraham
Lincoln (126), Diane Sawyer (129), Wilson Mizner (130),
Winefred Newman (134), Joseph Newton (135), Dennis
Rainey (136), Theodore Roosevelt (137), Leo Tolstoy
(138), Henry Ford (141), George Boardman (143), Jeremy
Taylor (144), Gary Smalley & John Trent (147).

Additional Copies of this book and other titles
in the *God's Little Instruction Book* series are
available from your local bookstore.

God's Little Instruction Book

God's Little Instruction Book for Couples

God's Little Instruction Book for Men

God's Little Instruction Book for Mom

God's Little Instruction Book for Teachers

God's Little Instruction Book for Women

If you have enjoyed this book,
or if it has impacted your life,
we would like to hear from you.

Please contact us at:

Honor Books

An Imprint of Cook Communications Ministries

4050 Lee Vance View

Colorado Sjprings, CO 80918

www.cookministries.com